Teacup Yorkie as Pets

A Complete Teacup Yorkie Owner's Guide

Teacup Yorkie Breeding, Where to Buy, Types, Care, Cost, Diet, Grooming, and Training all Included.

By: Lolly Brown

Foreword

Teacup Yorkie breed is the miniature version of the Yorkshire Terrier. Aside from its size, these Yorkshire Terrier dogs are coined "Teacup," by the Yorkshire Terrier Club of America solely for its members for the purpose of ethical reasons. Teacup Yorkies have a reputation for being very energetic, very bold and much more adorable than the normal sized Yorkshire Terrier. They are greatly admired as pets because of their "small but adorable" attitude.

Although Teacup Yorkie are truly a great choice as pets, these dogs doesn't come with a thin instruction manual, but fear not! In this book you'll be easily guided on understanding your Teacup Yorkie dog, their behaviors, their characteristics, how you should feed and care for them and a whole lot more.

Embark on a wonderful journey of sharing your life with a Teacup Yorkie. Learn to maximize the great privilege of living with one and be able to share this unique and unforgettable experience just like many pet owners that came before you!

Table of Contents

Introduction...1

   Glossary of Dog Terms 4

Chapter One: Teacup Yorkie in Focus..................................9

   Facts about Teacup Yorkie 10

      Quick Facts 13

   Teacup Yorkie Breed History 14

Chapter Two: Teacup Yorkie Requirements 17

   License Requirements..18

      United States Licensing for Dogs 18

      Licensing for Dogs in United Kingdom 19

   How Many Teacup Yorkie Should You Keep? 20

   Do Teacup Yorkie Get Along with Other Pets? 21

   Ease and Cost of Care 21

      Initial Costs..22

      Monthly Costs 28

   Pros and Cons of Teacup Yorkie 31

Chapter Three: Purchasing Teacup Yorkie...........................33

   Finding a Reputable Teacup Yorkie Breeder.............34

   Tips in Choosing a Reputable Breeder 34

   Rescue Dogs Adoption 37

   List of Breeders and Rescue Websites 37

Selecting a Healthy Teacup Yorkie 41

Tips on How to Dog-Proof Your Home 43

Chapter Four: Caring Guidelines for Teacup Yorkie 47

Ideal Habitat Requirements for Teacup Yorkie 48

Supplies and Equipment for Your Teacup Yorkie 49

Setting Up Your Teacup Yorkie's Crate 52

Chapter Five: Nutritional Needs of Teacup Yorkie 53

The Nutritional Needs of Dogs 54

How to Select a Healthy Dog Food Brand 56

Tips for Feeding Your Teacup Yorkie 59

Toxic Foods to Avoid 60

Chapter Six: Training Your Teacup Yorkie 63

Socializing Your Puppy 64

Tips in Training Your Teacup Yorkie 66

Tips in Housebreaking Your Teacup Yorkie Puppy 68

Chapter Seven: Grooming Your Teacup Yorkie 73

Recommended Tools for Grooming 74

Tips for Bathing and Grooming Teacup Yorkie 75

Other Grooming Tasks 77

Chapter Eight: Breeding Your Teacup Yorkie 81

Basic Dog Breeding Information 82

Mating Behavior of Dogs 82

Tips for Breeding Your Teacup Yorkie.................................84

Labor Process of Teacup Yorkie 86

Chapter Nine: Keeping Your Teacup Yorkie Healthy 89

Common Health Problems of Teacup Yorkie 90

Recommended Vaccinations for Teacup Yorkie.............106

Signs of Possible Illnesses..108

Teacup Yorkie Care Sheet 111

Basic Teacup Yorkie Information.......................................112

Habitat Requirements..113

Nutritional Needs...114

Breeding Information...115

Index...119

Photo Credits...127

References...129

Introduction

    A lot of breeders and first time dog owners are confused when experts say that there's no such thing as a Teacup Yorkie breed. Technically, Teacup Yorkies are Yorkshire Terriers that can fit in the size of a teacup, hence its name. It is the same breed with only a different size. So experts are correct, there is no separate breed for these dogs. You can still call them Yorkshire Terriers and be right about it, because the term "Teacup Yorkie" is only created by the Yorkshire Terrier Club of America solely for its members for the purpose of ethical reasons. So those Yorkshire terrier dogs that are way too small were considered as Teacup Yorkies.

The main difference though is that Teacup Yorkies are Yorkshire Terriers that are not qualified for showing; the AKC will not allow these small dogs to join competitions even if technically they are Yorkshire Terriers because they did not meet the standards of a normal size terrier type.

Teacup Yorkies are a unique breed not only in terms of their fluffy appearance but also mainly because their super cute size not to mention their affectionate attitude. These dogs are small yet so adorable! But what is it that makes these dogs so popular? There is no short answer to this question because, with Teacup Yorkie, there is just so much to love.

The Teacup Yorkie is more than just a pet; it is a loyal, protective and loving companion. These dogs are trainable, cuddly and energetic, plus they are very great family pets and relates well with children. If you are thinking about adopting a dog or purchasing a puppy, the Teacup Yorkie is definitely a great breed to consider. Before you bring a Teacup Yorkie home, however, you should be a responsible dog owner and learn everything you can about this breed and how to care for it properly.

Fortunately, this ultimate guide will teach you on how to be the best Teacup Yorkie dog owner you can be! Inside this book, you will find tons of helpful information about Teacup Yorkie dog; how they live, how to deal with them and realize the great benefits of owning one!

This book includes information about creating the ideal habitat and diet for your dog as well as tips for breeding and showing your Teacup Yorkie. You will also find in-depth health information for the breed including common health problems affecting it and the treatment options available.

The great world of Teacup Yorkie breed awaits! What are you waiting for? Keep reading!

Glossary of Dog Terms

AKC – American Kennel Club, the largest purebred dog registry in the United States

Almond Eye – Referring to an elongated eye shape rather than a rounded shape

Apple Head – A round-shaped skull

Balance – A show term referring to all of the parts of the dog, both moving and standing, which produce a harmonious image

Beard – Long, thick hair on the dog's underjaw

Best in Show – An award given to the only undefeated dog left standing at the end of judging

Bitch – A female dog

Bite – The position of the upper and lower teeth when the dog's jaws are closed; positions include level, undershot, scissors, or overshot

Blaze – A white stripe running down the center of the face between the eyes

Board – To house, feed, and care for a dog for a fee

Breed – A domestic race of dogs having a common gene pool and characterized appearance/function

Breed Standard – A published document describing the look, movement, and behavior of the perfect specimen of a particular breed

Buff – An off-white to gold coloring

Clip – A method of trimming the coat in some breeds

Coat – The hair covering of a dog; some breeds have two coats, and outer coat and undercoat; also known as a double coat. Examples of breeds with double coats include German Shepherd, Siberian Husky, Akita, etc.

Condition – The health of the dog as shown by its skin, coat, behavior, and general appearance

Crate – A container used to house and transport dogs; also called a cage or kennel

Crossbreed (Hybrid) – A dog having a sire and dam of two different breeds; cannot be registered with the AKC

Dam (bitch) – The female parent of a dog;

Dock – To shorten the tail of a dog by surgically removing the end part of the tail.

Double Coat – Having an outer weather-resistant coat and a soft, waterproof coat for warmth; see above.

Drop Ear – An ear in which the tip of the ear folds over and hangs down; not prick or erect

Entropion – A genetic disorder resulting in the upper or lower eyelid turning in

Fancier – A person who is especially interested in a particular breed or dog sport

Fawn – A red-yellow hue of brown

Feathering – A long fringe of hair on the ears, tail, legs, or body of a dog

Groom – To brush, trim, comb or otherwise make a dog's coat neat in appearance

Heel – To command a dog to stay close by its owner's side

Hip Dysplasia – A condition characterized by the abnormal formation of the hip joint

Inbreeding – The breeding of two closely related dogs of one breed

Kennel – A building or enclosure where dogs are kept

Litter – A group of puppies born at one time

Markings – A contrasting color or pattern on a dog's coat

Mask – Dark shading on the dog's foreface

Mate – To breed a dog and a bitch

Neuter – To castrate a male dog or spay a female dog

Pads – The tough, shock-absorbent skin on the bottom of a dog's foot

Parti-Color – A coloration of a dog's coat consisting of two or more definite, well-broken colors; one of the colors must be white

Pedigree – The written record of a dog's genealogy going back three generations or more

Pied – A coloration on a dog consisting of patches of white and another color

Prick Ear – Ear that is carried erect, usually pointed at the tip of the ear

Puppy – A dog under 12 months of age

Purebred – A dog whose sire and dam belong to the same breed and who are of unmixed descent

Saddle – Colored markings in the shape of a saddle over the back; colors may vary

Shedding – The natural process whereby old hair falls off the dog's body as it is replaced by new hair growth.

Sire – The male parent of a dog

Smooth Coat – Short hair that is close-lying

Spay – The surgery to remove a female dog's ovaries, rendering her incapable of breeding

Trim – To groom a dog's coat by plucking or clipping

Undercoat – The soft, short coat typically concealed by a longer outer coat

Wean – The process through which puppies transition from subsisting on their mother's milk to eating solid food

Whelping – The act of birthing a litter of puppies

Chapter One: Teacup Yorkie in Focus

Teacup Yorkies may often time look like a cute baby, your witty seatmate, your loyal friend, your playful sibling or that very adorable kid you always wanted. In whatever attitude or mood it appeals, you can expect it to be confident, adventurous, brave, and a caring devoted pet you've always dreamed of.

The Teacup Yorkie is a designer breed of dog that is irresistibly cute and sassy but it may not be the right choice for everyone. Before you decide whether or not it might be the right pet for you and your family, you need to learn and invest a significant amount of time in getting to know these animals.

In this chapter you will receive an introduction to the Teacup Yorkie breed including some basic facts and information as well as the history of how it came about. This information, in combination with the practical information about keeping Teacup Yorkie dogs in the next chapter, will help you decide if this is the perfect dog companion for you.

Facts about Teacup Yorkie

These dogs are very fragile and should be handled with care! Seriously. Everyday activities can easily harm and injure these little breed.

The body of a Teacup Yorkie is neat, compact and well proportioned. They usually have black, medium - sized eyes that are not too prominent, coupled with ears that are small and V - shaped. They have a long and straight coat, sometimes a curly one that is usually hypoallergenic because it is common among small terrier types. The most common colors for the Teacup Yorkie breed include Black and Gold, Black and Tan, Blue and Gold.

The Teacup Yorkie was developed as a toy breed which may not come as a surprise because of their small teacup sized bodies, but before they became house pets of aristocrats back in the day, they were originally owned by the working class particularly the weavers, in which they serve as a rat catcher, and their fine long silky coats are used as looms.

Teacup Yorkies protect and serve as a watchdog as well. Just like normal sized Yorkshire terriers they are fond of barking and they also have a reputation for being brave and very playful. The Teacup Yorkie is a very intelligent dog and a highly trainable breed; they are not easily fooled and they only trust people with whom they form very strong bonds with.

Teacup Yorkies are way bolder and confident than normal sized terriers; their size won't stop them in doing what they want. They can also be witty at times when left to their own devises. Proper socialization and training from a young age will help prevent the Teacup Yorkie from being suspicious of new people and excessive barking. They do very well as family pets but are not advised for families with very young children 7 years old and below.

This breed is fond of attention and constantly seeks affection from their owners; they are ideal as first pets but like other dogs, have a tendency to have unstable, aggressive temperaments which can be also dangerous to innocent strangers, that's why socialization and training at an early age is highly recommended.

The Teacup Yorkie stands no more than 5 - 6 inches tall at maturity and there is only a slight difference in size between males and females of the breed. Unlike normal sized terriers, these dogs weigh only between 2 and 4 pounds! Since the Teacup Yorkie is a very active and agile dog – some say much more than the normal terrier, it has a great deal of energy and may need a fair amount of exercise to work off that energy although it doesn't necessarily require regular or excessive amount of exercise. It can adapt to almost any kind of environment – it can fit in a teacup!! This is why they are also perfect for owners who live in apartments, although you might want to consider its loud barking for your neighbor's sake. They are generally curious yet controllable indoors as long as they get enough mental and physical stimulation during the day and have proper house training.

The average lifespan for these breed is about 12 years the only downside is that they are not that healthy compared to normal terrier types. It is very prone to health issues common in smaller breeds such as birth defects, Patellar Luxation and anesthesia complications. They frequently suffer from it.

Quick Facts

Pedigree: Terrier dog breed

AKC Group: Toy Group

Breed Size: Small

Height: 5 - 6 inches (5–10 cm) for females and males

Weight: average of 2 pounds; maximum of 4 pounds

Coat Length: long and straight coat can also be curly

Coat Texture: gloss, fine and silky

Color: Black and Gold, Black and Tan, Blue and Gold

Markings: Gold Mask, Tan Mask

Ears: small, V-shaped and erect

Tail: short to medium-length

Temperament: active, friendly, loyal, bold, confident

Strangers: may be wary around strangers

Other Dogs: generally good with other dogs if properly trained and socialized; may tend to launched itself to larger dogs

Other Pets: friendly with other pets but if not properly introduce may result to potential aggression

Training: intelligent and can be trained

Exercise Needs: very active; doesn't require regular or excessive amount of exercise

Health Conditions: not that healthy very prone to patellar luxation, PSS, cataracts, retinal detachment, dry eye, corneal dystrophy, keratitis, hypoglycemia, and progressive retinal atrophy

Lifespan: average 12 years

Teacup Yorkie Breed History

During the mid – 19th century, particularly around 1860's, a breed of dog called the Waterside Terrier was brought to Yorkshire, England by immigrants who were weavers from Scotland. The Waterside Terrier is the Yorkie's ancestral breed which was formed by crossing an old rough – coated Black and Tan English Terrier (that are common in Manchester) with a Paisley and Clydesdale terriers.

In 1872, Yorkies entered the United States and around 1878. Yorkies had become a fashionable pet breed during the late Victorian era and even years before that.

The term "Teacup Yorkie" is only created by the Yorkshire Terrier Club of America solely for its members for the purpose of ethical reasons. They are not recognized as an individual breed and therefore not qualified for showing; they do not meet the requirements of a terrier type breed.

Today, more dog enthusiasts and pet lovers wanted Teacup Yorkie, sometimes even more than the normal size Yorkshire terriers because it's much smaller and well much more adorable.

Chapter Two: Teacup Yorkie Requirements

Are you now thinking of getting a Teacup Yorkie dog? Awesome! After knowing what they are, their behaviors, and how to deal with them, it's time to give you practical tips on what you need to know before buying one.

In this chapter, you will get a whole lot of information on its pros and cons, its average associated costs as well as the licensing you need so that you will be well on your way to becoming a legitimate Teacup Yorkie pet owner – should you decide to be one! It's up to you! Read on!

License Requirements

If you are planning to acquire a Teacup Yorkie as your pet, there are certain restrictions and regulations that you need to be aware of. Licensing requirements for pets varies in different countries, regions, and states.

In the United States there are no federal requirements for licensing dogs or even cats – these rules are regulated at the state level. While it is true that most states do not have a mandatory requirement for people to license their dogs, it is always a good idea to do so because it will not only serve as protection for your pet but also for you.

Here are some things you need to know regarding the acquirement of Teacup Yorkie dogs both in United States and in Great Britain.

United States Licensing for Dogs

As mentioned earlier, there are no federal requirements for licensing dogs in the United States they are only determined at the state level. Licensing requirements vary from one state to another, but most states do require dog owners to register and license their dogs.

In order to obtain a license for your dog you will have to provide proof that your dog has been vaccinated against rabies.

Once you obtain the license you will then have to renew it each year along with your dog's rabies vaccination. Dog licenses only cost about $25 (£16.25) per year, which is not a big expense. There might be additional requirements that need to be submitted in other states. The license will be considered temporary status until all documents are received.

Even if your state or region does not require you to license your dog, it is still a good idea to do so. If your dog escapes or gets lost, having him properly identified will significantly increase the chances of you finding him. A dog license is attached to an identification number which is linked to you – if someone finds your dog; they will be able to find your contact information through the license. You can also add an ID tag to your dog's collar along with his license for good measure.

Licensing for Dogs in United Kingdom

In UK, licensing requirements for pets are a little different than they are in the United States. In the United Kingdom, it is mandatory for dog owners to license their dogs. The main difference, however, is that British dog owners do not need to vaccinate their dogs against rabies because the disease has been eradicated. Dog licenses are renewed annually and they are not a significant expense.

In some cases you will need to get a special permit if you plan to travel with your dog into or out of the country.

How Many Teacup Yorkie Should You Keep?

There are several important factors you need to consider when answering this question. The question is do you have the space and the financial ability to provide for more than one dog? Teacup Yorkie are small, and generally a low maintenance breed but they still require a good deal of time and attention – think carefully before buying more than one of them. If you do have the time and money to care for another dog, your Teacup Yorkie might appreciate having another dog of its kind around to keep him company while you are away.

Ideally one or two Teacup Yorkie dogs are fine; just make sure that before you get another one, you can provide for the needs of both dogs. As long as you socialize your Teacup Yorkie from a young age, they shouldn't have trouble getting along with each other or with other dogs.

Do Teacup Yorkie Get Along with Other Pets?

For the most part, Teacup Yorkie get along with other pets as long as they have been properly socialized from a young age, however these dogs as small as they are, are not aware of their own size that's why they tend to launch themselves towards bigger dogs such as Golden Retriever, Cane Corso etc. In order to prevent potentially disastrous consequences, introduce your dog to larger dogs under supervision, before they interact on their own. It is also important to note that huge dogs shouldn't be around smaller ones because they seem them as prey.

If you are going to have other household pets around such as cats, it is wise to properly introduce them and also monitor their interaction to make sure they're getting along. Be more cautious when introducing strangers, even if dogs are man's best friend, they still might be sensitive to new faces, so do it properly.

Ease and Cost of Care

Owning a Teacup Yorkie doesn't come cheap! The fact that these dogs are a designer breed requires a need to provide supplies and be able to cover the expenses in order to maintain a healthy lifestyle and environment for your pet.

These things will definitely add up to your daily budget, and the cost will vary depending on where you buy it; the brand of the accessories, the nutrients included in its food and the time being. If you want to seriously own a Teacup Yorkie as a pet you should be able to cover the necessary costs it entails.

In this section you will receive an overview of the expenses associated with purchasing and keeping a Teacup Yorkie dog such as food and treats, grooming and cleaning supplies, toys, veterinary care, and other costs so that you can determine whether you are able to provide for such a dog or not.

Initial Costs

The initial expenses associated with keeping Teacup Yorkie as pets include the cost of the dog itself as well as its crate, accessories, toys, initial vaccinations, micro-chipping or licensing, spay/neuter surgery and also grooming supplies. You will find an overview of these costs below as well as the estimated total expense for keeping Teacup Yorkie:

Purchase Price: average price of $1,200 - $1,500 (£940.11 - £1175.13)

The cost to purchase a Teacup Yorkie will vary depending on the breed you choose and where you get it. Some breeders will also require a minimum amount of deposit. It is always best to purchase from a reputable breeder because it will reduce the risk for your dog developing an inherited disease. Keep in mind that the cost highly depends on the quality of the breed. If you choose to adopt, expect additional adoption fees as well. There could also be additional charges if your pet will be shipped, it can add up to the price of your puppy to some extent.

Crate: average $30 (£19.50)

Having a crate for your Teacup Yorkie puppy is very important. Not only will it be used during housetraining, but it will also give your dog a space of his own where he can relax if he wants to. You'll need to purchase a fairly small crate for your Teacup Yorkie puppy and you might need to buy a larger one once he reaches full size, although even if she does, it may still be naturally small compared to other dog breeds.

Food/Water Bowls: total cost of $20 (£18)

In addition of providing your Teacup Yorkie dogs with a crate to sleep in, you should also make sure it has a set of high-quality food and water bowls. The best materials for these is stainless steel because it is easy to clean, cannot be easily chewed or eaten and won't acquire bacteria, another good option is ceramic.

Toys: total cost of $50 (£32.50)

Like other pets, Teacup Yorkie needs plenty of stimulation to keep their intelligent and curious minds entertained. Keep dog boredom at bay with fun toys for your dogs.

To start out, plan to buy an assortment of toys for your dog until you learn what kind it prefers. Total cost of toys may reach approximately $50 or more, again costs may vary depending on the brand. If your dog likes to destroy toys, you may need to set aside an additional amount of money to buy more toys.

Microchipping: $30 (£19.50)

In the United States and United Kingdom there are no federal or state requirements saying that you have to have your dog micro-chipped, but it is very ideal, as mentioned earlier, your Teacup Yorkie could slip outside through an open door or window without you noticing it. If someone finds it without identification, they can take it to a shelter to have its microchip scanned.

A microchip is something that is implanted under your dog's skin and it carries a number that is linked to your contact information. The procedure takes just a few minutes to perform and it only costs about $30 on average, but in some states cost may vary and there are certain documents that you may need to submit in your local government.

Initial Vaccinations: $50 (£32.50) or more

During the first year of life, your Teacup Yorkie puppy will need a variety of different vaccinations. If you purchase your puppy from a reputable breeder, he will probably already have had a few of these. Over the first few weeks after you bring your puppy home, however, he will need more. You should budget a substantial amount for initial vaccinations just to be prepared. Also if your dog has the appropriate boosters it needs, at a young age, it can definitely lengthen their life expectancy.

Spay/Neuter Surgery: $50 - $200 (£32.50 - £130)

If you don't plan to breed your Teacup Yorkie you should have it neutered (for males) or spayed (for females) before 6 months of age. In females, this procedure includes surgically removing the ovaries and usually the uterus while in males, the testicles are surgically removed.

Spaying or neutering your pet decreases the likelihood of certain types of cancers and eliminates the possibility of your pet producing an unwanted offspring. The cost for this surgery will vary depending where you go and on the gender of your dog. If you go to a traditional veterinary surgeon, the cost for spay/neuter surgery could be very high but you can save money by going to a veterinary clinic. The average cost for neuter surgery is $50 to $100 and spay surgery costs about $100 to $200.

Supplies/Accessories: average $35 (££32.50)

There will be times that you may need to let your Teacup Yorkie to play outside the house. You might also need several dog accessories like a leash (if you're planning to train them or walk them outside) and other things like grooming materials during shows or simply repairing dog supplies. On average, extra accessories may cause at least $35 depending on brand and quality of the product.

An overview of these costs is provided for you in on the next section. Costs may vary depending on brand as well as location and the current exchange rate.

General Expenses Overview

Needs	Costs
Purchase Price	$1,200 - $1,500 (£940.11 - £1175.13)
Crate	$30 (£19.50)
Food/Water Bowl	$20 (£18)
Toys	$50 (£32.50)
Microchipping	$30 (£19.50)
Vaccinations	$50 (£32.50)
Spay/Neuter	$50 to $200 (£32.50 - £130)
Accessories	$35 (£32.50)
Total	$1,465 to $1,765 (£1,147.71 – £1,382.74)

Monthly Costs

The monthly costs associated with keeping a Teacup Yorkie can also be quite expensive. Some of the things that need to be bought on a monthly basis are food and treats, annual license renewal, toy replacements, and veterinary exams. Provided in this section is an overview of each of these costs as well as an estimate for each cost.

Food and Treats: total of $50 (£32.50)

Feeding your Teacup Yorkie a healthy diet is very important for its health and wellness, especially for a very active and huge pet. A high-quality diet for dogs may not be cheap and highly depends on the brand. The right amount of nutrients should be provided to maintain its healthy and appealing physique. You should be prepared to spend around $40 for a high-quality dog food which will last you about a month. You should also include a monthly budget of at least $10 for treats, that way he/she can be rewarded every time he/she did a good job in training or behaving.

Grooming Costs: approximately $9 to $12.50 (£8 - £11.25)

You should plan to have your Teacup Yorkie professionally groomed about twice a year in order to keep his skin and coat in good health. You should budget about $10.50 (£8 - £11.25) per month.

License Renewal: average of $2.00 (£1.30)

The cost to license your Teacup Yorkie is generally about $20 and you can renew the license for the same price each year, some states may cost more. License renewal cost divided over 12 months is about $2 per month.

Veterinary Exams: approximately $7.00 (£4.55)

In order to keep your Teacup Yorkie healthy you should take him to the veterinarian at least twice a year; keep in mind that you may need to take him more often while he is a puppy to give him the vaccines he needs. The average cost for a vet visit is about $40 (£26) so, if you have two visits per year, it averages to about $7 (£4.55) per month.

Additional Costs: $15 (£9.75)

In addition to the cost for food, grooming, license renewal, and vet visits you will have to cover other costs on occasion. These costs may include replacements for toys, a larger collar as your puppy grows, cleaning products, and more. You won't have to cover these costs every month but you should include it in your budget to be safe.

An overview of these costs is provided for you in on the next section. Costs may vary depending on brand as well as location and the current exchange rate.

Monthly Expenses Overview

Needs	Monthly Costs
Food and Treats	$50 (£32.50)
Grooming Costs	$9 to $12.50 (£8 - £11.25)
License Renewal	$2 (£1.30)
Veterinary Exams	$7 (£4.55)
Other Costs	$15 (£9.75)
Total	$83 to $95.50 (£68.09 – £78.34)

Pros and Cons of Teacup Yorkie

Before you bring a Teacup Yorkie home you should take the time to learn the pros and cons of the breed. Every dog breed is different so you need to think about the details to determine whether the Teacup Yorkie is actually the right pet for you.

In this section you will find a list of pros and cons for the Teacup Yorkie dog breed:

Pros for the Teacup Yorkie Breed

- A small and cute dog breed that is perfect for apartments and even houses with no yards
- Confident and bold yet generally people - oriented even with strangers
- Most miniature breed of dogs like the Teacup Yorkie has hypoallergenic coat that is suited for allergic or sensitive owners
- Doesn't require extensive exercises
- Compared to other hybrids, Teacup Yorkie is much smaller and generally a low maintenance pet
- Coat is fairly easy to care for with regular brushing and combing, they are a non to low – shredder breed

- Makes a good watch dog that can protect you or your family
- Generally good with other family pets such as cats
- Very loyal and funny, forms strong bonds with family
- Friendly and easy-going breed as long as it is properly socialized
- It can be ideal as a first pet
- A truly great companion

Cons for the Teacup Yorkie Breed

- Has a tendency to launch themselves at larger dogs which can cause injuries
- A small dog who loves to bark constantly and consistently; proper training is needed from day 1!
- Not recommended for homes with very young children
- Can destroy house furniture when bored or left alone too much
- May suffer from separation anxiety when left for a long period of time
- Can be aggressive and wary towards people when not raised or properly trained
- A dog who is sometimes stubborn and witty
- Can be prone to sickness inherited from its parent breed.

Chapter Three: Purchasing Teacup Yorkie

Now that you are already aware and have prior knowledge about the legal aspects of owning and maintaining a Teacup Yorkie as well as its pros and cons, the next step is purchasing one through a local pet store or a legitimate breeder. In this chapter you will find valuable information about where to find a Teacup Yorkie breeder, how to select a reputable breeder, and how to choose a healthy puppy from a litter. You will also receive tips for puppy-proofing your home and for introducing your new Teacup Yorkie puppy to your family.

Finding a Reputable Teacup Yorkie Breeder

Once you've decided that the Teacup Yorkie is the right dog for you, your next step is to find one. Purchasing a Teacup Yorkie might be as easy as stopping in to your local pet store since it is such a popular breed, but you should ask yourself whether this is really the best option. Many pet stores receive their puppies from puppy mills – organizations which breed dogs as quickly as they can, keeping the dogs in squalid conditions. As a result of irresponsible breeding practices, the puppies are often malnourished or suffering from health problems. The best way to make sure you get a Teacup Yorkie puppy in good health is to do your research and to purchase one from a reputable Teacup Yorkie breeder.

Tips in Choosing a Reputable Breeder

The difference between a reputable breeder and a puppy producer is that the former spends large amounts of time and money on the best interest of the breed, while the latter is often motivated by profit. However, in order to find a good Teacup Yorkie breeder, you may have to do some research first. Once you've compiled a list of several Teacup Yorkie breeders you then need to go through them to choose the best option. You don't want to run the risk of purchasing a puppy from a hobby breeder or from someone who doesn't follow responsible breeding practices. Keep in mind that when you purchase a Teacup Yorkie puppy you are making a 12 year commitment!

Here are the following things you need to do to help you find a reputable Teacup Yorkie breeder:

- Ask around at veterinary offices, groomers, and pet stores for referrals to Teacup Yorkie breeders and assemble as much information as you can about each one.

- Visit the website for each breeder (if they have one) and check to see if the breeder is registered with a national or local breed club

- Contact each breeder individually and ask them questions about their knowledge of the Teacup Yorkie breed as well as their breeding experience.

- Ask specific questions about the breeder's program and the dogs used to produce the puppies. Ask what the breeder does to prevent the passing of congenital conditions to the puppies.

- Remove the breeders from your list who do not seem to be knowledgeable about the breed or if they seem to be just hobby breeders looking to make a buck.

- Eliminate breeders from your list who refuse to answer your questions or who do not seem genuinely concerned for the wellbeing of their puppies.

- Schedule a visit with several breeders and ask for a tour of the facilities – check to make sure they are clean and that the dogs look healthy.

- Narrow down your list of breeders and make your selection – you should also ask about the breeder's preferences for putting down a deposit on a puppy.

- Place your deposit to reserve a puppy – in the next section you will receive tips for choosing a puppy from a litter.

Rescue Dogs Adoption

As an alternative to purchasing a Teacup Yorkie puppy from a legitimate breeder, you should also consider adopting a rescue dog. Not only will you be doing your part in the war against puppy mills, but you will be providing a homeless dog with a loving home and new lease on life. There are many benefits associated with adopting a rescue dog and you might even be able to find a purebred Teacup Yorkie or a Teacup Yorkie puppy.

Adoption is much more affordable than purchasing a purebred puppy from a breeder and the dog is likely to have already been housebroken and may also have some amount of obedience training as well.

List of Breeders and Rescue Websites

In this section, you'll be given recommended websites on reputable breeders as well as rescue dogs associations in United States and United Kingdom, once you have narrow down your list of breeders, you can go and check to see the best option for you.

U.S. Teacup Yorkie Breeders

Tiny Puppy
<http://www.tinypuppy.com/>

Pocket Puppies
<http://www.pocketpuppies.com/>

Good Puppie
<http://www.goodpuppie.com/>

Karen's Yorkies
<http://www.karensyorkies.com/>

Texas Tiny Yorkies
<http://www.texastinyyorkies.com/>

Chocolate Bark Kennel
<http://www.chocolatebarkkennel.com/>

Puppy Heaven
<http://www.puppyheaven.com/>

Wendy's Yorkie
<http://www.wendysyorkies.com/>

Pocket Book Pups
<http://www.pocketbookpups.net/>

Teacup Puppies Store
<http://www.teacuppuppiesstore.com/>

Yorkie Babies
<http://www.yorkiebabies.com/teacuppuppies.html>

Sissy J's Poochies
<http://www.sissyjspoochies.com/sale.html>

U.S. Teacup Yorkie Recues

Humane Society Organization
<http://www.humanesociety.org/>

Yorkie 911 Rescue
<http://www.yorkie911rescue.com/>

Save a Yorkie Rescue
<http://www.saveayorkierescue.org/>

Yorkie Haven Rescue
<http://www.yorkiehavenrescue.com/adoptable.php>

Adopt-a-Pet
<http://www.adoptapet.com/s/adopt-a-yorkie?>

U.K. Teacup Yorkie Breeders

Pexswillow Dogs UK
<http://www.pexswillowdogs.co.uk/small-crossbreeds>

GumTree

<https://www.gumtree.com/dogs/uk/teacup>

PreLoved UK

<http://www.preloved.co.uk/classifieds/pets/dogs/all/uk/teacup+puppies>

U.K. Teacup Yorkie Rescues

Dog's Trust

<https://www.dogstrust.org.uk/>

Blue Cross UK

<https://www.bluecross.org.uk/>

Royal Society for the Prevention of Cruelty to Animals UK

<https://www.rspca.org.uk/home>

Little Dog Rescue UK

<http://www.littledogrescue.co.uk/index.html>

Many Tears Rescue UK

<http://www.manytearsrescue.org/>

Selecting a Healthy Teacup Yorkie

Teacup Yorkie on average can live for up to 12 years and more!! These breed are long time companions, and its longevity highly depends on how your chosen breeders took care of them especially when they were young. This section will give you simple tips on how you can spot a healthy Teacup Yorkie puppy that you can keep for life!

- **Behavior:** Puppies should be active and playful, and loves to interact with people or with other pets. Play with the puppies to get a feel for their individual temperaments then pick the one that suits you best.

- **Ability:** Find a puppy that can run or walk normally, and does not have any mobility issues.

- **Dealing with Humans:** Pick up a puppy and hold him to see how he responds to human contact. Look for signs that the puppies are nervous or fearful of people; they shouldn't run away or hide when you approach them.

- **Puppy Interaction:** Step back and observe the puppies as a litter. Watch how they interact with each other and make sure they display normal puppy behavior.

- **Appetite:** If possible, watch the puppies being fed to make sure they have a healthy appetite and no problems eating solid food.

- **Body Appearance**: Examine the puppies' body for signs of any illness and potential injury. There should be no swelling or discoloration on the body.

- **Coat:** The texture of the puppy's coat should be smooth and has a fine texture. Look for any signs of fleas or any other pests within its coat.

- **Eyes:** The eyes should be clear and bright with no discharge.

- **Ears:** The ears should be clean and clear with no discharge such as wax or filmy material or signs of inflammation.

- **Mouth and Teeth:** Look out for any excessive drooling or unusual discharge.

- **Belly or Stomach:** Look out for a distended or swollen tummy area. Also make sure there are no lumps or unusual curves around the belly.

- **Anal Area:** The anal area should be clean. Try lifting the puppy's tail gently and look for any signs of diarrhea.

Important Note

A reputable breeder won't let you take home a puppy that is younger than 8 weeks. Some states even have laws which prohibit the sale of puppies less than 8 weeks of age. It is important to wait until the puppy is fully weaned and eating solid food before you bring him home.

Tips on How to Dog-Proof Your Home

Teacup Yorkie, like any other dogs are curious by nature, so it's important to dog-proof your house before bringing home your new pet, not only for its safety but also yours. Here are some tips on how to prepare your home for your new found pet:

- Place all of your food in tightly lidded containers and store them in the cupboard or pantry.

- Make sure your trashcan has a tight-fitting lid and store your garbage out of your puppy's reach.

- Pick up small objects from the floor and put them away – this includes things like toys, rubber bands, pieces of string, etc.

- Store all of your medications (prescription and over-the-counter) safely in a medicine cabinet.

- Keep all of your cleaning supplies stored away where your puppy can't get into them – this includes supplies kept in the garage.

- Remove any toxic houseplants from your home or move your plants so they are well out of your puppy's reach.

- Check to make sure none of the plants on your property are toxic to dogs – if they are, remove them or fence them off so your puppy can't get into them.

- Cover any open bodies of water that could pose a drowning hazard for your puppy – this includes toilets, sinks, ponds, pools, and more.

- Make sure all of the outlets in your home are protected by plastic covers.

- Tie up the cords for your blinds as well as electric cords so your puppy can't chew on them.

These are just a few of the many things you should do to keep your puppy safe at home and keep your home intact! After going through the items on this list, walk around your house and view things from your puppy's eyes – remove anything that he might be tempted to chew on or play with that could be harmful.

Chapter Four: Caring Guidelines for Teacup Yorkie

The Teacup Yorkie makes a wonderful pet largely due to his confident yet adorable personality, but these dogs are also very adaptable to different types of living situations. In this chapter you will find some basic information about cultivating a happy and healthy home life for your Teacup Yorkie. You will find tips for setting up your Teacup Yorkie's crate as well as valuable information about making sure your Teacup Yorkie's exercise needs are met.

Ideal Habitat Requirements for Teacup Yorkie

The great thing about Teacup Yorkie is that they don't take up too much space to roam around with, but aside from space, the main thing your Teacup Yorkie needs in terms of its habitat is lots of love and affection from his human companions and adequate daily exercise. Even though the Teacup Yorkie is sometimes stubborn and witty, it is a very loyal and affectionate breed that bonds closely with family, so you should make an effort to spend some quality time with your Teacup Yorkie each and every day. If your Teacup Yorkie doesn't get enough attention he may be more likely to develop problem behaviors like chewing or excessive barking and potential aggression as well as separation anxiety.

In addition to playing with your Teacup Yorkie and spending time with him every day, you also need to make sure that his needs for exercise are met. The Teacup Yorkie doesn't require extensive exercises but it is still recommended to take your dog for a walk or run once in a while plus some active play time, this is very important for your Teacup Yorkie. You should also make sure your Teacup Yorkie gets plenty of mental stimulation from interactive toys and games.

Supplies and Equipment for Your Teacup Yorkie

In order to care for your Teacup Yorkie properly you will need to have certain supplies on hand. Most importantly, your Teacup Yorkie needs a crate or carrier to sleep in because you will also use it for housetraining. Your dog will also need food and water dishes and other accessories.

Below is the list of required supplies and accessories for your dog:

- Crate or carrier
- Blanket or dog bed
- Food and water dishes
- Toys (assortment)
- Collar, leash and harness
- Grooming supplies

Crate or Carrier

Having a crate or carrier for your Teacup Yorkie serves two important functions. First, it will give your Teacup Yorkie a place to sleep as well as a place to retire to if he needs some time to himself. Second, it will play an important role in housebreaking your Teacup Yorkie. Choose a carrier that is just large enough for your Teacup

Yorkie to comfortably stand up, turn around, sit, and lie down in. You may need to purchase one crate for your Teacup Yorkie as a puppy and upgrade it once he reaches full size.

Blanket or Dog Bed

To make your Teacup Yorkie's crate more comfortable you will need to line it with a soft blanket or pet bed. Choose something that is comfortable but also easy to wash. While your Teacup Yorkie is being housebroken, you might even want to get something waterproof.

Food/Water Dishes

Food and water dishes for dogs come in all shapes and sizes but you should choose a set that suits your dog's needs. Teacup Yorkie are a large-breed dog, so don't choose anything relatively small. As mentioned in the previous chapters, stainless steel and ceramic bowls do not harbor bacteria like plastic can and they are easy to clean.

Toys

In order to keep your Teacup Yorkie occupied you will need to provide him with an assortment of toys. Making sure your Teacup Yorkie has plenty of toys will keep him from chewing on your furniture and it will give you something to use in playing with him.

Collar, Leash and Harness

Having a collar for your Teacup Yorkie is incredibly important because you will need to attach your dog's license and ID tag to it. Choose a collar appropriate for your Teacup Yorkie's size – it should fit well without being too tight or too loose. Choose a leash that won't weigh your Teacup Yorkie down during walks and consider investing in a harness as well. Harnesses offer improved control over your dog's movements and they take the pressure off your dog's neck and throat.

Grooming Supplies

In order to keep your Teacup Yorkie's skin and coat in good health you'll need to brush and comb him several times a week. Have a soft brush on hand as well as wide-toothed comb. You may also want to buy an undercoat rake to help remove dead hairs from your Teacup Yorkie's coat before he sheds them all over your furniture.

Once you have assembled all of these items you can use them to create a living space for your Teacup Yorkie. You will find tips for setting up your Teacup Yorkie's crate in the next section of this book.

Setting Up Your Teacup Yorkie's Crate

Once you have assembled all the necessary supplies you can set up your Teacup Yorkie's crate. It is a good idea to set up your dog's crate in an area that gives him some space to call his own.

Here are some tips on how to set up a crate:

- Choose a room that isn't in the center of the action, but it shouldn't be too secluded either.
- The location should offer enough space for you to set up a puppy play pen in addition to your dog's crate and supplies.
- Place the crate in the play pen or build a wall around the area surrounding the crate to create your own pen.
- Make sure you place your puppy's food and water bowls nearby as well as a box of his toys.

Chapter Five: Nutritional Needs of Teacup Yorkie

Time for feeding! Feeding your Teacup Yorkie is not that hard. However, its level of activity should be taken into consideration to meet its nutritional diet. They're sometimes choosy eaters so it is highly recommended that dogs, like many other pets, should be given the right amount of recommended food for a balanced nutrition because proper diet can lengthen the life expectancy of your dog.

In this section, you'll learn the majority of your pet's nutritional needs as well as feeding tips and foods that are good and harmful.

The Nutritional Needs of Dogs

Like all living things, dogs require a balance of protein, fats, and carbohydrates in their diet as well as certain vitamins and minerals. When you think about the proper diet for dogs, you probably already know that meat plays an important role. This is true, but you should not overlook the other nutrients your dog needs.

In this section you will find an overview of the nutrients essential to your dog's diet and where they come from:

Carbohydrate

Dogs do not have specific requirements for carbohydrate in their diet, but carbohydrates do provide dietary fiber as well as valuable vitamins and minerals. Your dog should get his carbohydrate from whole grains like brown rice or oatmeal – these are the most digestible sources. Gluten-free and grain-free alternatives like sweet potato and tapioca are also good choices. Just be sure to avoid low-quality carbohydrates made from corn and soy ingredients because they provide very little nutritional value – dog food companies just use them to add bulk to their products without increasing cost or nutritional value.

Fats

Fat is the most highly concentrated source of energy available to your dog. Like protein, fats should come from animal-based sources like chicken fat and fish oil instead of plant-based sources like flaxseed or canola oil. You should make sure your Teacup Yorkie gets a balance of omega-3 and omega-6 fatty acids to ensure proper skin and coat health.

Protein

Protein is made up of amino acids and it is incredibly important for the growth and development of your Teacup Yorkie's tissues, organs, and cells. Dogs require animal-based proteins like fresh meat and meat meals because it provides them with the essential amino acids they cannot produce on their own. Plant-based proteins are less biologically valuable for your dog, though they are not essentially harmful.

Vitamins

Your dog needs to get certain vitamins from his diet because his body cannot produce them on his own. The most important vitamins for dogs are vitamin D, vitamin A, vitamin C and vitamin E.

Minerals

Minerals are inorganic compounds, because of that your dog's body cannot synthesize them; it must come from his diet. The most important minerals for dogs include copper, calcium, phosphorus, potassium, sodium, and iron.

Water

In addition to macronutrients and micronutrients, your Teacup Yorkie also needs plenty of fresh water on a daily basis. About 70% of your dog's bodyweight is made up of water so, if he doesn't drink enough water during the day, it can have a serious negative impact on his health.

How to Select a Healthy Dog Food Brand

Now that you have a basic understanding of your Teacup Yorkie's nutritional needs you can think about shopping for a high-quality dog food. Your Teacup Yorkie should be fed a high-quality dry kibble dog food that is specially formulated for small-breed dogs. It is highly recommended that you mixed a tiny amount of canned food into the kibble to entice your Teacup Yorkie to eat. Without dry food, the Teacup Yorkie has a great potential to develop gum disease, bad breath and tooth loss. You don't want that do you?

Many dog food companies offer formulas for puppies as well as adults, so choose the formula that is right for your Teacup Yorkie, depending on his age.

Shopping for dog food can be difficult because there are so many different options to choose from. In order to separate the high-quality foods from the low-quality foods, you need to learn how to read a dog food label. When comparing dog foods, the first thing you want to look for is the AAFCO statement of nutritional adequacy – this will tell you that the product meets the basic nutritional needs of dogs. AAFCO is the American Association of Feed Control Officials and the statement of nutritional adequacy will look something like this:

"[Product Name] is formulated to meet the nutritional levels established by the AAFCO Dog Food nutrient profiles for [Life Stage]."

After you've determined that the product is approved by AAFCO, you can then take a more detailed look at the ingredients list. Remember, protein is the most important nutritional consideration for dogs so you should look for a high-quality source of protein (or two) at the top of the ingredients list. Ingredients lists for dog foods are assembled in descending order by volume – this means that the ingredients at the top of the list are present in the highest quantities. So, if a product lists something like deboned chicken or fresh turkey as the first ingredient, you can assume that the product is a good source of protein.

When perusing dog food labels, you are likely to come across meat meals like chicken meal or salmon meal. The word "meal" might turn you off, but it is actually a very good ingredient to have in a dog food. Fresh meats contain up to 80% water so, by the time the product is cooked, the actual volume of the meat is much lower than it was originally. Meat meals have already been cooked down to a moisture level around 10% so they are actually a much more concentrated source of protein than fresh meat.

In addition to high-quality proteins, you should also look for digestible carbohydrates like whole grains and fresh vegetables. Things like brown rice and oatmeal are valuable additions to a commercial dog food while products like corn gluten meal or wheat flour are not. Gluten-free and grain-free carbohydrates like sweet potato and tapioca starch are also good ingredients if you are looking for a product that is free from gluten and grains. Just try to avoid byproduct meals as well as corn and soy ingredients. When it comes to fats, you should look for animal-based fats like chicken fat and salmon oil – these are much more biologically valuable to your dog than plant-based fats like canola oil or flaxseed. You should look for a blend of both omega-3 and omega-6 fatty acids as well.

Not only do you need to be mindful of the ingredients included in your dog's food, but you should also be mindful of things that are NOT included. Avoid products made with artificial preservatives like BHT and BHA. You also want to look for products free from artificial flavors, colors and dyes. If your Teacup Yorkie suffers from food allergies, consider a Limited Ingredient Diet (LID) which is made with a novel source of protein that won't trigger his allergies. Novel sources of protein might include things like bison, venison, or even kangaroo meat.

Tips for Feeding Your Teacup Yorkie

When it comes to feeding your Teacup Yorkie, you may be wondering how much food is too much. The Teacup Yorkie is one of the many breeds prone to obesity and once your dog becomes obese it can be difficult for him to lose weight. Your best bet is to follow the feeding recommendations on the dog food package as a starting place. Follow the feeding recommendations for a few weeks and keep an eye on your Teacup Yorkie's weight. If he starts to gain weight, you may need to cut back on his portions a little bit. If your dog loses weight or doesn't appear to have as much energy as he used to, you may need to feed him a little bit more.

Another important thing to consider in feeding your Teacup Yorkie is how many times you should feed him per day.

While your Teacup Yorkie is still a puppy, you might be able to feed him freely instead of rationing his meals. Just keep in mind that your Teacup Yorkie puppy will reach his maximum size more quickly, at which point you should switch him to an adult dog food formula. Monitor your Teacup Yorkie puppy's growth and once he reaches about 80% of his maximum expected size, make the switch. Your veterinarian should be able to help you estimate your Teacup Yorkie's maximum size.

Toxic Foods to Avoid

It might be tempting to give in to your dog when he is begging at the table, but certain "human foods" can actually be toxic for your dog, just as dog foods can be poisonous to human beings. As a general rule, you should never feed your dog anything unless you are 100% sure that it is safe. In this section you will find a list of foods that can be toxic to dogs and should therefore be avoided.

- Alcohol
- Apple seeds
- Avocado
- Cherry pits

- Chocolate
- Coffee
- Garlic
- Grapes/raisins
- Hops
- Macadamia nuts
- Mold
- Mushrooms
- Mustard seeds
- Onions/leeks
- Peach pits
- Potato leaves/stems
- Rhubarb leaves
- Tomato leaves/stem
- Xylitol
- Walnuts
- Yeast Dough

If your Teacup Yorkie eats any of these foods, contact the Pet Poison Control hotline right away at (888) 426 – 4435.

Chapter Six: Training Your Teacup Yorkie

At some point in time, you and your pet will already get along and are comfortable in each other, strengthen your relationship by training them. Training a Teacup Yorkie is not that hard to do, in fact it can be a fun and rewarding bonding experience for both of you.

There are lots of pet owners out there who have properly trained and raised a well-behaved Teacup Yorkie. Even if they are only a designer breed, they are smart and can be taught to follow a human, that is why they can absorb information very quickly and easily as long as you do it right.

Trust is the most important key in training your dog or puppy. The first thing you need to do is to be able to establish a solid connection and rapport between you and your pet.

This chapter will provide some guidelines you can do to get your dog to be well-behaved and disciplined. Are you ready? Read on!

Socializing Your Puppy

The first few weeks of your Teacup Yorkie puppy's life are incredibly important. Not only is this when you will establish a bond with him, but it is also when he is the most impressionable. Socialization is essential for puppies when they are young because the experiences they have during this impressionable period will determine who they are as an adult.

If your puppy isn't properly socialized, he might turn into a shy and timid adult dog who responds to new people and unfamiliar situations with fear or uncertainty instead of normal curiosity. Fortunately, socialization for Teacup Yorkie dogs is easy to grasp.

Here are some tips on how to socialize your dog so that it'll feel confident and at ease with others:

- Introduce your puppy/dog to friends in the comfort of your own home where your puppy/dog feels safe.

- Take your dog with you to the pet store or to a friend's house so that it experiences new locations.

- Expose your puppy/dog to people of different sizes, shapes, gender, and skin color.

- Introduce your puppy/dog to children of different ages. Just supervise the kids to make sure they handle the puppy/dog safely.

- Take your puppy/dog with you in the car when you run errands, make them part of your daily routine as much as possible.

- Expose your puppy/dog to loud noises such as fireworks, cars backfiring, loud music, and thunder. It will get used to it eventually.

- Introduce your puppy/dog to various appliances and tools such as blenders, lawn mowers, vacuums, etc.

- Play with your puppy/dog using different kinds of toys and experiment with different kinds of food and treats to also see its preferences.

Tips in Training Your Teacup Yorkie

In addition to socializing your new Teacup Yorkie puppy you should also begin training as soon as possible. Teacup Yorkie are very intelligent and eager to learn, although at times they may be witty and halfhearted so starting with training early will increase your chances of having a well-behaved and obedient adult dog. When it comes to dog training, there are many different methods to choose from. Some of the most popular methods include positive reinforcement, punishment, alpha dog, and clicker training.

In the section you will find an overview of each training method below:

Positive Reinforcement

This method of training hinges on your dog's natural desire to please. In essence, you train your dog to repeat desired behaviors by rewarding him for doing them. For example, if you want your dog to sit when you give him the "Sit" command, teach him what the command means and then reward him each time he responds to the command appropriately. Positive reinforcement training is one of the most popular and effective dog training methods.

Clicker Training

This type of training is a version of positive reinforcement training and it is highly popular. The key to success with positive reinforcement training lies in helping your dog to identify the desired behavior – that is where the clicker comes in. You go through the normal process of training, giving your dog a command and guiding him to perform the desired behavior. Then, as soon as he displays the behavior you click the clicker and immediately issue a reward – this helps your dog to learn more quickly which behavior it is that you desire.

You should only use the clicker during the first few repetitions of a training sequence until your dog learns what the desired behavior is – you don't want him to become dependent on the clicker to perform that behavior.

Punishment

This type of training is almost the opposite of positive reinforcement training – rather than rewarding your dog for performing desired behaviors, you punish him for performing unwanted behaviors. The punishment used doesn't have to be violent or cruel – it can be as simple as withdrawing your attention to teach your dog to stop whining.

Give your dog the opposite of what he wants to curb the negative behavior in question. This type of training is more effective as a method for curbing negative behaviors than for teaching positive behaviors.

Alpha Dog

This type of training was made popular by the Dog Whisperer, Cesar Milan. According to Milan, he believes that dogs are natural pack animals and that dog owners must establish themselves as the leader of the dogs "pack". This means that you must make your dog submissive to you so he will submit to your will. Alpha dog training involves things like never letting the dog walk through the door before you, or waiting to feed your dog until after you have eaten. Although this training method works for some people, it is not endorsed by the ASPCA and other animal rights groups.

Tips in Housebreaking Your Teacup Yorkie Puppy

After socialization, housetraining is probably one of your most important tasks as a dog owner. While your Teacup Yorkie puppy is still young, he will not be physically capable of holding his bladder or bowel movements. Making sure to take your puppy outside very frequently (as often as once an hour) will help to reduce the frequency of accidents until your puppy is old enough for housetraining. The most effective method for housetraining a puppy is crate training.

Here are some useful tips for housetraining your puppy:

- Follow the guidelines provided earlier in this book to choose a crate for your puppy and set it up as directed.

- Get your puppy used to the crate by tossing treats into it and feeding him his meals in the crate.

- Eventually your puppy should be comfortable enough with the crate to take naps in it with the door open.

- Start closing the door to the crate while your puppy is inside and leave him there for a few minutes.

- Gradually increase the length of the confinement until your puppy can remain calm in the crate for at least 30 minutes.

- Start housetraining by selecting a certain area of the yard where you want your puppy to do his business.

- Take your puppy to that area each time you take him outside and give him a verbal command like "go pee".

- When your puppy does his business in the area, praise him excitedly and offer a reward to reinforce the behavior.

- Keep your puppy in the same room as you at all times when you are at home and supervise him closely.

- Take your puppy outside every hour or two, especially after naps and within 30 minutes after a meal.

- If your puppy does not do his business when you take him out, take him right back inside and try again in 30 minutes.

Important Note

When you are not at home or unable to watch your puppy, confine him to the crate – avoid leaving any food or water which might increase his risk for having an accident.

Be reminded of the following:

- Be sure not to leave your puppy in the crate for longer than he is physically capable of holding his bladder and bowels.

- Gradually increase the length of the time your puppy spends in the crate until he can make it overnight.

- Always take your puppy outside immediately after releasing him from the crate and before you put him in it.

Chapter Seven: Grooming Your Teacup Yorkie

Your Teacup Yorkie's skin produces natural oils that help to protect its coat and keep it moisturized. Grooming for dogs is not just about keeping it clean, it is mainly about improving and maintaining the condition of the skin. Grooming your dog helps to distribute its natural body oils to keep his skin healthy, shiny, and soft. No matter what kind of coat your Teacup Yorkie has, it is your job to groom it properly so it remains in good health.

In this chapter you will learn the basics about grooming your Teacup Yorkie – this includes brushing and bathing your dog as well as trimming his nails, cleaning his ears, and brushing his teeth.

Recommended Tools for Grooming

The coat of Teacup Yorkie varies tremendously since Teacup Yorkie is a result of crossbreed. It may be curly, wavy or straight, the great part is that they don't shred a lot which means you will not need to do very much maintenance – brushing a few times a week and bathing as needed should be sufficient. Nevertheless, it is essential that you have the right tools on hand to complete the job.

Here is a list of several recommended grooming tools and supplies below:

- Soft brush
- Metal comb
- Undercoat rake
- Small, sharp scissors
- Dog-friendly shampoo
- Nail clippers
- Dog-friendly ear cleaning solution
- Dog toothbrush
- Dog-friendly toothpaste

As long as you have these supplies on hand you should be able to do most of your Teacup Yorkie's grooming yourself at home. Still, you might want to have your Teacup Yorkie professionally groomed twice a year for good measure.

Tips for Bathing and Grooming Teacup Yorkie

Now that you know what tools and supplies you need to have on hand for grooming your Teacup Yorkie you are ready to learn the process. You should brush your Teacup Yorkie's coat as often as possible – at least once a day is recommended to keep your dog's skin and coat soft and silky. Another characteristic of Teacup Yorkie which is also common to miniature dogs, is that they produce little dander, which is actually an advantage for allergic owners.

The first step in grooming your Teacup Yorkie is to go over his body with a metal comb. Start at the back of the head and work your way down the dog's neck and back, brushing in the direction of hair growth. Move on to the dog's sides and comb the fur down each leg. Once you've gone over your Teacup Yorkie with a comb to remove tangles you can do it again with the wire pin brush to collect loose and dead hairs. If for some reason your Teacup Yorkie is a particularly high shedder (most Yorkie breeds blow their coats twice a year) you may also want to use an undercoat rake to remove dead hairs from the Teacup Yorkie's undercoat before they can be shed.

After you've gone over your Teacup Yorkie with the comb and brush he is ready for bathing. Keep in mind that the Teacup Yorkie doesn't need to be bathed frequently –

you should only do it when he really needs it. If you bathe your dog too frequently it could cause his skin and coat to dry out. When you do bathe your dog, be sure to use dog-friendly shampoo that will be gentle on his skin.

Here are some guidelines for bathing your Teacup Yorkie:

- Place a non-slip mat or towel on the bottom of your tub then fill it with a few inches of warm water (not hot water).

- Put your Teacup Yorkie in the tub and use a handheld sprayer or a container to wet down his coat as thoroughly as possible.

- Apply a small amount of your dog-friendly shampoo to your hand then work it into your Teacup Yorkie's coat, forming a thick soapy lather.

- Work the soap through the hair on your dog's neck, back, legs, chest and tail – avoid getting his ears, eyes, and nose wet.

- Thoroughly rinse away the soap using clean water until all traces have been removed.

- Use a damp washcloth to carefully clean the fur on your dog's head and face, if necessary, keeping the eyes and ears dry.

- Towel-dry your Teacup Yorkie using a large fluffy towel until you have already removed as much moisture from his coat as possible.

- If it is cold out and your Teacup Yorkie is shivering, finish drying his coat using a hairdryer on the low heat setting.

The most important thing to remember when bathing your Teacup Yorkie is that you must keep his ears dry. Wet ears are a breeding ground for bacteria and infection. The Teacup Yorkie usually have erect and floppy ears that allow plenty of airflow to the ear canal, that's why there is a huge risk for ear infections so be very careful.

Other Grooming Tasks

In addition to brushing and bathing your Teacup Yorkie, you also need to engage in some other grooming tasks including trimming your dog's nails, cleaning his ears, and brushing his teeth.

Brushing Your Teacup Yorkie's Teeth

The idea of brushing your dog's teeth might sound gross but it is actually a very important part of grooming. Periodontal (dental) disease is incredibly common among pets and it can actually lead to some serious health problems including tooth loss, heart disease, and organ damage.

Here are some simple tips on how to brush your dog's teeth and mouth:

- Place a small amount of dog-friendly toothpaste on a dog toothbrush.
- Brush just a few of your dog's teeth at a time until he gets used to the process.
- Be sure to reward your dog after brushing his teeth so he learns that good behavior earns him a treat. This will make things much easier for you in the long run.

Cleaning Your Teacup Yorkie's Ears

Cleaning your Teacup Yorkie's ears isn't a difficult task, but he might not like it. A dog's ears are a breeding ground for bacteria so, if you do not keep them clean, your dog may have an increased risk for recurrent ear infections.

Here are some simple tips on how to brush your dog's teeth and mouth:

- Clean your dog's ears, add a few drops of a dog-safe ear cleaning solution to your dog's ear canal.
- Massage the outside of your Teacup Yorkie's ears by hand to spread the solution.
- Use clean cotton balls to clean away any buildup inside your dog's ears (as well as excess cleaning solution).
- Let your dog's ears dry.

Trimming Your Teacup Yorkie's Nails

When it comes to trimming your dog's nails, you need to be very careful. Each of your dog's nails contains a quick – the blood vessel that supplies blood to the nail. If you cut the nail too short and sever this blood vessel it could not only hurt your dog, but it could cause profuse bleeding as well. The best way to prevent this from happening is to make sure you have the right tool and to learn the proper nail trimming procedure before you do it yourself. Ask your vet or a professional groomer to show you how to trim your dog's nails and then, when you do it yourself, be sure to only trim away the sharp tip.

Chapter Eight: Breeding Your Teacup Yorkie

If you decided to buy two dogs, for instance a male and female and keep them together, you should definitely prepare for the possibility of breeding, unless it's the same gender, otherwise you're going to be caught off guard! If you are interested in breeding your Teacup Yorkie, this chapter will give you a wealth of information about the processes and phases of its breeding and you will also learn how to properly raise puppies on your own. This not for everyone but if you want to have better understanding about how to raise these dogs, then you should definitely not miss this part! On the contrary if you are interested in becoming a reputable breeder, then this is a must read chapter for you.

Basic Dog Breeding Information

When it comes to dog breeding, no matter what breed you choose, you need to be absolutely sure of your decision before you begin. Breeding dogs of any breed is a huge responsibility and it can take a financial toll on your family as well. Unfortunately, many dog owners out there think that breeding their dogs is a good way to make some extra money. The reality is, however, that by the time you pay for healthcare costs for your pregnant female and a litter of puppies (not to mention food and housing for all of them), you will be lucky to come out even.

If you do not plan to breed your Teacup Yorkie, the ASPCA recommends having him or her neutered or spayed before 6 months of age. For female dogs, they should be spayed before their first heat. Keep in mind that spaying and neutering dogs before 6 months of age can significantly reduce their risk for certain types of cancer and other serious diseases.

Mating Behavior of Dogs

The most important thing you need to learn about is the estrus cycle. This is the cycle also known as "heat" through which female dogs goes about twice a year. The cycle lasts for 14 to 21 days on average and it occurs about every 6 months once it becomes regular – it can take a few years for a dog to establish a regular cycle.

Swelling of the vulva for females - dogs may also excrete a bloody discharge at the start of the cycle, though many dogs do not develop this until the 7th day of the cycle. As your Teacup Yorkie's cycle progresses, the discharge will become lighter in color until it is pink and watery by the 10th day of the cycle. In addition to this discharge, many female dogs start to urinate more frequently during their cycle – they might also develop urine marking behavior to attract male dogs.

A male dog can smell a female in heat from very great distances, so you need to be very careful to keep your female Teacup Yorkie indoors while she is in heat. When you take her outside, be sure to keep her on a leash and supervise her closely. Never take a female dog in heat to the dog park or to another location where intact male dogs may be present. If you intend to breed your Teacup Yorkie, you want to avoid any accidental mating.

When the discharge from your dog's vulva becomes light in color and watery, this is likely when she will be the most fertile and when she will begin to ovulate – this generally happens around day 11 to 15 of the cycle. It is during this time that you want to introduce her to the male dog to make an attempt at breeding. If you introduce the dogs too early in the female's cycle she might not be receptive to him. If she isn't, just wait another day or two before trying again. Your Teacup Yorkie is technically capable of conceiving at any point during her cycle because the sperm from the male dog can survive in the reproductive tract for as long as 5 days.

Tips for Breeding Your Teacup Yorkie

Now that you know the basics about breeding dogs you can learn the specifics about Teacup Yorkie. The Teacup Yorkie has a gestation period lasting about 58 - 68 days (or about 9 to 10 weeks). The gestation period is the period of time following conception during which the puppies develop in the mother's uterus. The average litter size for the Teacup Yorkie breed is between 1 to 5 puppies, they have smaller litter size compare to larger Yorkie breeds. Keep in mind that new mothers will often have smaller litters – the next few litters will generally be larger before the litter size starts to taper off again.

Again, the Teacup Yorkie gestation period lasts about 65 to 68 days but you won't be able to tell that your Teacup Yorkie is pregnant right away. By the 28th day of pregnancy or during the fourth week, it is safe to perform an ultrasound on the pregnant dog, and most likely your vet will confirm that your dog is indeed pregnant because around the 28th to 32nd day, your veterinarian will be able to feel the puppies by palpating the mother's uterus.

To increase your chances of a successful breeding, you need to keep track of your Teacup Yorkie's estrus cycle. Once your female reaches the point of ovulation, you can introduce her to the male dog and let nature take its course. Breeding behavior varies slightly from one breed to another, but you can expect the male dog to mount the female from behind (as long as she is receptive). If the breeding is successful, conception will occur and the gestation period will begin.

While the puppies are developing inside your female Teacup Yorkie's uterus, you need to take special care to make sure the female is properly nourished. You do not need to make changes to your dog's diet until the fourth or fifth week of pregnancy. At that point you should slightly increase her daily rations in an amount proportionate to her weight gain. It is generally best to offer your dog free feeding because she will know how much she needs to eat. Make sure your dog's diet is high in protein as well as calories and fat to support the development of her puppies – calcium is also very important.

<u>Signs that your dog is pregnant:</u>

- Fast nipple growth or appearance
- Less energetic
- More affectionate or clingy
- Experiences mood swings
- The stomach will expand and get firm
- The dog will clean herself more than the usual
- May attempt to build a dog's nest.

Labor Process of Teacup Yorkie

By the eighth week of pregnancy you should start preparing yourself and your dog for the whelping. This is the time when you should set up a whelping box where your female dog can comfortably give birth to her puppies. Place the box in a quiet, dim area and line it with newspapers and old towels for comfort. The closer it gets to the whelping, the more time your dog will spend in the whelping box, preparing it for her litter.

During the last week of your Teacup Yorkie's pregnancy you should start taking her internal temperature at least once per day – this is the greatest indicator of impending labor. The normal body temperature for a dog is about 100°F to 102°F (37.7°C to 38.8°C). When your dog's body temperature drops, you can expect contractions to begin within 24 hours or so. Prior to labor, your dog's body temperature may drop as low as 98°F (36.6°C) – if it gets any lower, contact your veterinarian.

Once your Teacup Yorkie starts going into labor, you can expect her to show some obvious signs of discomfort. Your dog might start pacing restlessly, panting, and switching positions. The early stages of labor can often last for several hours and contractions may occur as often as 10 minutes apart. If your Teacup Yorkie has contractions for more than 2 hours without any of the puppies being born, contact your veterinarian immediately. Once your dog starts giving birth, the puppies will arrive about every thirty minutes following ten to thirty minutes of straining.

After each puppy is born, the Teacup Yorkie will lick the puppy clean; it may even eat the umbilical cord because it is animal instinct. This also helps to stimulate the puppy to start breathing on his own. Once all of the puppies have been born, the mother will expel the rest of the placenta (the afterbirth) and then let the puppies start nursing. It is essential that the puppies begin nursing within one hour of being born because this is when they will receive the colostrum from the mother. Colostrum is the first milk produced and it contains a variety of nutrients as well as antibodies to protect the pups until their own immune systems have time to develop. In addition to making sure that the puppies are feeding, you should also make sure that the mother eats soon after whelping.

Teacup Yorkie puppies are small in size; these puppies are also born blind, with their eyes and ears closed, so they are completely dependent on the mother for several weeks. Around 3rd week, the puppies will open their eyes and their ears will become erect sometime after. As the puppies grow, they will start to become increasingly active and the will grow very quickly as long as they are properly fed by the mother.

At six weeks of age is the time you should begin weaning the puppies by offering them small amounts of puppy food soaked in water or broth. The puppies might sample small bits of solid food even while they are still nursing and the mother will general wean the puppies by week 8, with or without your help. If you plan to sell the puppies, be sure not to send them home unless they are fully weaned at least 8 weeks old. You should also take steps to start socializing the puppies from an early age to make sure they turn into well-adjusted adults.

Chapter Nine: Keeping Your Teacup Yorkie Healthy

As mentioned earlier, Teacup Yorkie often has health issues and they are vulnerable to diseases. You as the owner should be aware of the potential threats and diseases that could harm the wellness of your Teacup Yorkie. Just like human beings, you need to have knowledge on these diseases so that you can prevent it from happening in the first place. You will find tons of information on the most common problems that may affect your cat including its causes, signs and symptoms, remedies and prevention.

Common Health Problems of Teacup Yorkie

In this section, you will learn about the diseases that may affect and threaten your Teacup Yorkie's wellness. Learning these diseases as well as its remedies is vital for you and your dog so that you could prevent it from happening or even help with its treatment in case they caught one.

Below are some of the most common health problems that can occur to Teacup Yorkie dogs. You will learn some guidelines on how these diseases can be prevented and treated as well as its signs and symptoms.

Legg-Calvé-Perthes Disease

This condition is commonly seen in miniature, toy, and small-breed dogs and it usually common during five to eight months of age. This disease involves spontaneous degeneration of the head on the femur bone, located in the dog's hind leg. This results in disintegration of the hip joint (coxofemoral) and bone and joint inflammation.

Causes

The exact cause of Legg-Calvé-Perthes Disease is unknown, but researchers suggest that dogs suffering because from this condition, have blood supply issues to the femoral head.

Signs and Symptoms

If you notice your dog showing lameness for two to three months; he is carrying its affected limbs or has pain when moving its hip joint, as well as wasting its thigh muscles on its affected limbs these are signs that your dog is suffering from this disease.

Diagnosis and Treatment

You will need to give a thorough medical history of your dog's health, including duration and frequency of symptoms. Laboratory testing is not usually required to diagnose the disease. Your vet will most likely recommend your dog for X-rays of the affected area, which should identify any changes in the femoral bone and joint. Upon further diagnosis the widening of joint space, decreased bone density, and thickening of femoral bone neck can be seen during its early stages. In advanced cases, extreme deformation of femoral head, new bone formation in the affected area, and femoral neck fracture may also be seen.

The veterinarian may also perform a complete physical examination on your dog, particularly the affected limb and hip joint area.

Patellar Luxation in Dogs

Patellar luxation is another common disease in toy and miniature dog breeds. This occurs when the dog's kneecap (patella) is dislocated from its normal anatomic position in the groove of the thigh bone (femur). Female dogs are usually the ones affected by these disease more than male dogs.

When the kneecap is dislocated from the groove of the thigh bone, it can only be returned to its normal position once the quadriceps muscles in the hind legs of the animal relax and lengthen. It is for this reason that most dogs with the condition will hold up their hind legs for a few minutes.

Causes

The main cause of Patellar Luxation or a dislocated kneecap is genetic malformation or trauma. This condition can normally be seen approximately four months after birth.

Signs and Symptoms

Usually, a dog with a dislocated kneecap will exhibit prolonged abnormal hind limb movement, occasional skipping or hind limb lameness, and sudden lameness. The specific symptoms of a dislocated kneecap will depend on the severity and persistence of the condition, as well as the amount of degenerative arthritis that is involved.

Diagnosis and Treatment

Veterinarians will usually suggest performing Craniocaudal (top view) and Mediolateral (side view) X-rays for the stifle joint, hip, and hock as well as skyline X-rays for the thigh bone. Your vet will also likely perform an examination by touch to feel for kneecap freedom.

The Craniocaudal and Mediolateral tests will detect the bending and twisting of the thigh bone and larger bone of the lower leg while Skyline X-rays may reveal a shallow, flattened, or curved groove of the thigh bone.

Aside from X-rays, a fluid sample may also be taken from the joint and an analysis of the lubricating fluid in the joint may show a small increase in mononuclear cells.

Portosystemic Shunt (PSS)

This condition is an abnormal connection between the portal vascular system and systemic circulation.

In a healthy dog, the blood that exits the intestines, spleen, and pancreas enters the portal vein, which then takes blood to the liver. The liver metabolizes and detoxifies this blood. If a shunt is present, the liver is deprived of factors that enhance liver development, these are called hepatotrophic factors; blood from the abdominal organs which should be drained by the portal vein into the liver is instead shunted to the systemic circulation by the PSS which results in failure of the liver to reach normal size (hepatic atrophy).

This means that a portion of the toxins, proteins and nutrients absorbed by the intestines bypass the liver and are shunted directly into the systemic circulation.

2 Types of Congenital Shunts
- Extrahepatic (outside the liver)
- Intrahepatic (inside the liver)

Signs and Symptoms:

Below are the common signs and symptoms of PSS, these are often episodic and are usually seen after eating. These neurological signs are due to the hepatic encephalopathy syndrome.

- ataxia (abnormal swaying)
- blindness
- head pressing
- loss of appetite or anorexia
- vomiting
- diarrhea
- seizures
- constipation
- excessive urination/drinking
- difficulty urinating
- blood in the urine or hematuria

Diagnosis

If your veterinarian confirms or suspects that your dog has PSS, he/she will advised that your dog undergo several tests and full diagnostic work-up such as blood work, urinalysis, liver function tests, radiographs, ultrasound, nuclear scintigraphy (a non-invasive technique involving colonic administration of a radioisotope), portography (X-ray dye study that specifically highlights the portal system and a CT scan.

Some of these diagnostics may be completed by your primary care veterinarian, but for its treatment and other extensive tests, you will be referred to an ACVS board-certified veterinary surgeon or veterinary specialty center.

Treatment

The only treatment for this condition is surgery; however, before undergoing surgery, your dog may need medical management to improve its health to a point where the risk of anesthesia and surgery is low. In order to medically stabilize your dog before surgery, a low protein diet and oral administration of antibiotics and lactulose will be done. The goals are to decrease the bacterial population in the intestines and to minimize the production of toxins.

Once your dog is medically stabilized, the next step is for him/her to undergo surgical attenuation (narrowing) or full ligation (tying off) of the abnormal shunt vessel for a single PSS. This full ligation may be done instantaneously using suture material or intra-venous injection of an embolus of special glue material, or delayed full ligation with an ameroid constrictor, cellophane band or an intra-venous embolic coil.

Your primary care veterinarian may refer you and your pet to an ACVS board-certified veterinary surgeon because this surgery is technically challenging and could be fatal as well.

Idiopathic Epilepsy

Epilepsy is a seizure disorder that may manifest in several different ways. In most cases, seizures are preceded by a focal onset phase during which the dog may appear dazed or frightened.

Signs and Symptoms

The dog typically falls to its side and becomes stiff, salivating profusely and paddling with all four limbs. Seizures generally last for 30 to 90 seconds and they most commonly occur while the dog is resting or asleep.

Two Types of Epilepsy:

- **Primary epilepsy** is also called true epilepsy or idiopathic epilepsy – this type of epilepsy involves seizure with an unknown cause. This condition usually presents between 6 months and 5 years of age and it may have a genetic link.

- **Secondary epilepsy** - a condition in which the cause of the seizures can be determined.

Causes and Diagnosis

As mentioned earlier, the primary epilepsy has no cause, it is most likely hereditary. The most common causes for secondary epilepsy include degenerative disease, developmental problems, toxins/poisoning, infections, metabolic disorders, nutritional deficiencies, and trauma.

Veterinarians use information about the age of onset and pattern of the seizures to make a diagnosis.

Treatments

Treatment options for canine epilepsy may involve anticonvulsant medications and monitoring of the dog's health and weight.

Hip Dysplasia

Hip dysplasia is a very common musculoskeletal problem among dogs. In a normal hip, the head of the femur (thigh bone) sits snugly within the groove of the hip joint and it rotates freely within the grove as the dog moves. Hip dysplasia occurs when the femoral head becomes separated from the hip joint – this is called subluxation. This could occur as a result of abnormal joint structure or laxity in the muscles and ligaments supporting the joint.

This condition can present in puppies as young as 5 months of age or in older dogs.

Causes and Diagnosis

Genetics are the largest risk factor for hip dysplasia, though nutrition and exercise are factors as well. Diagnosis for hip dysplasia is made through a combination of clinical signs, physical exam, and x-rays.

Signs and Symptoms

The most common symptoms of hip dysplasia include pain or discomfort, limping, hopping, or unwillingness to move. As the condition progresses, the dog's pain will increase and he may develop osteoarthritis. The dog may begin to lose muscle tone and might even become completely lame in the affected joint.

Treatments

Surgical treatments for hip dysplasia are very common and generally highly effective. Medical treatments may also be helpful to reduce osteoarthritis and to manage pain.

Degenerative Myelopathy

Degenerative myelopathy is a progressive disease which affects the spinal cord in older dogs. This disease typically manifests between 8 and 14 years of age, beginning with loss of coordination in the dog's hind limbs.

Causes and Diagnosis

This disease is caused by degeneration of the white matter in the dog's spinal cord. This degeneration may or may not be caused by the mutation of a certain gene. In order to diagnose your Teacup Yorkie with degenerative myelopathy your veterinarian will perform tests to rule out other causes of the weakness. These tests may include MRI, myelography, and biopsy of the spinach cord. In many cases, however, the diagnosis cannot be completely confirmed except with an autopsy (necropsy).

Signs and Symptoms

At first the dog will wobble when walking or drag the feet – this might occur in one limb or both. As the disease progresses, the limbs become increasingly weak and the dog might have difficulty standing. Eventually, the weakness will worsen to the point of paralysis and the dog will be unable to walk.

Treatments

Unfortunately, there are no treatments available to slow or stop the progression of degenerative myelopathy. The best treatment is to manage the dog's symptoms and to keep him as comfortable as possible. The use of harnesses and carts is common for dogs that have lost the use of their hind limbs.

Glaucoma

The Teacup Yorkie breed is prone to several eye-related conditions including glaucoma. Glaucoma is a very common condition in which the fluid inside the dog's eye builds and creates intraocular pressure that is too high. When the pressure inside the eye increases, it can lead to damage of the internal structures within the eye. If this condition is not treated promptly, it can lead to permanent loss of vision or total blindness for the dog.

Signs and Symptoms

Glaucoma can sometimes be difficult to diagnose in the early stages, but common signs include dilated pupil, cloudiness of the eye, and rubbing the eye. If you notice any of these symptoms, seek immediate treatment.

Treatments

Treatment options include topical solutions to reduce pressure, increase drainage, and to provide pain relief.

Hypothyroidism

This condition is very common in dogs and it can produce a wide variety of symptoms. Hypothyroidism occurs when the thyroid gland fails to produce enough thyroid hormone – this often leads to weigh loss as well as hair and skin problems. Fortunately, this condition is easy to diagnose with a blood test that checks the dog's levels of certain thyroid hormones like T4.

The thyroid is a gland located in your dog's neck close to the voice box, or larynx. The activity of the thyroid is regulated by the pituitary gland in the brain which produces thyroid stimulating hormone (TSH).

Signs and Symptoms

The main symptoms of this disease include lethargy, hair loss, weight gain, excessive shedding, hyper-pigmentation of the skin, slow heart rate, high blood cholesterol and anemia.

Causes and Diagnosis

Hypothyroidism occurs when the thyroid produces insufficient thyroid hormone – this is most often caused by a destruction of the thyroid gland. This is often associated with other diseases like cancer or atrophy of the thyroid tissue. The use of certain medications can affect the thyroid gland as well. Hypothyroidism is most commonly diagnosed in dogs between 4 and 10 years of age.

Treatments

Treatment usually involves daily treatment with synthetic thyroid hormone.

Von Willebrand's Disease

Von Willebrand's disease (or vWD) is a disease of the blood that affects certain dog breeds more than others. This disease is caused a deficiency of von Willebrand Factor (vWF) in the dog's blood. Von Willebrand Factor is a type of adhesive glycoprotein found in the blood which is required for normal platelet binding, or clotting.

Signs and Symptoms

Lack of vWF can lead to excessive bleeding following even a minor injury. It may also cause nosebleeds, bloody urine, bloody stool, bleeding gums, and vaginal bleeding (in females). It can also cause bruising and anemia.

Causes and Diagnosis

This disease is an inherited condition caused by genetic mutations that affect the synthesis, release and stability of vWF. In order to diagnose vWD, your veterinarian will perform a physical exam as well as a medical history. Blood count and blood chemical profiles will also be obtained along with a urinalysis and electrolyte panel.

Treatment

A transfusion with fresh plasma and fresh blood to increase the supply of vWF in the blood is the best treatment for this disease. Fortunately, this condition can be managed in mild to moderate cases. Dogs with more severe vWD may require additional transfusions for surgery and supportive care may be required following spontaneous bleeding episodes.

Intervertebral Disk Disease

Intervertebral disk disease (IVDD) is another musculoskeletal issue common in Teacup Yorkie. This condition causes a wide variety of different symptoms ranging from mild pain to completely paralysis – it can also mimic the presentation of other musculoskeletal problems which can delay diagnosis. IVDD can occur in any breed, though it is more common in certain breeds including the Teacup Yorkie.

Signs and Symptoms

The symptoms of IVDD are highly variable and may include neck pain or stiffness, back pain or stiffness, abdominal tenderness, arched back, lameness, sensitivity to touch, stilted gait, reluctance to rise, loss of coordination, tremors, collapse, and paralysis. These symptoms most commonly present after strenuous activity of physical trauma. The most common cause of this condition is related to a disorder of cartilage formation called chondrodystrophy and it usually presents in dogs aged 3 to 6 years old.

Treatment

There are both medical and surgical treatment options available for intervertebral disk disease. Medical treatments may involve corticosteroids or non-steroidal anti-inflammatories aimed to treat pain and control inflammation. Surgical treatments may help to decompress the spinal cord or to inject enzymes to help stabilize the affected disks.

<u>Progressive Retinal Atrophy</u>

Another eye problem known to affect the Teacup Yorkie breed is progressive retinal atrophy, or PRA. This condition affects more than 100 different breeds and it is generally an inherited condition passed on through the genes. PRA affects the retina of the eye, the part that receives light and converts it into electrical nerve signals that the brain interprets as vision. Dogs with PRA typically experience arrested retinal development (called retina dysplasia) or early degeneration of the photoreceptors in the eye. Dogs with retinal dysplasia usually develop symptoms within 2 months and are often blind by 1 year.

Signs and Symptoms

The signs of PRA vary according to the rate of progression. This disease is not painful and it doesn't affect the outward appearance of the eye. In most cases, dog owners notice a change in the dog's willingness to go down stairs or to go down a dark hallway – PRA causes night blindness which can progress to total blindness.

Recommended Vaccinations for Teacup Yorkie

Like other dog breeds, Teacup Yorkie, as healthy as they are, can still catch different bacterial and viral infections once in a while; having your Teacup Yorkie vaccinated is the best way to protect him from common canine diseases like distemper and parvovirus fortunately it can be prevented through vaccination.

It is important to have your puppy vaccinated at an early age and to follow your vet's recommendations for annual booster shots. The vaccination recommendations listed below for your dog highly depends on the availability in your area, your dog's age, and any other risk factors specific to its lifestyle.

In this section you will learn the vaccination schedule that your puppy or dog may need, but be sure to consult the veterinarian for further instructions.

Vaccination Schedule for Dogs			
Vaccine	**Doses**	**Age**	**Booster**
Rabies	1	12 weeks	annual
Distemper	3	6-16 weeks	3 years
Parvovirus	3	6-16 weeks	3 years
Adenovirus	3	6-16 weeks	3 years
Parainfluenza	3	6 weeks, 12-14 weeks	3 years
Bordatella	1	6 weeks	annual
Lyme Disease	2	9, 13-14 weeks	annual
Leptospirosis	2	12 and 16 weeks	annual
Canine Influenza	2	6-8, 8-12 weeks	annual

Consult with your local veterinarian to determine the appropriate vaccination schedule for your dog. Remember, recommendations vary depending on the age, breed, and health status of the dog, the potential of the dog to be exposed to the disease, the type of vaccine, whether the dog is used for breeding, and the geographical area where the dog lives or may visit.

Signs of Possible Illnesses

- **Sneezing** - does your dog have nose discharge?
- **Dehydration** - does your dog drink less than the usual? It may be a sign that there is something wrong with your dog
- **Obesity** - is your dog showing signs of obesity? It may be prone to a heart disease, or diabetes. Monitor your dog's weight before it's too late.
- **Elimination** - does your dog regularly urinate and defecate? Always check its litter to make sure that its stool and urine is normal. Contact the vet immediately if there are any signs of bleed and diarrhea.
- **Vomiting** - does your dog vomits and is it showing signs of appetite loss?

- **Coat** - does its coat and skin still feel soft, firm and rejuvenated? If your dog is sick sometimes, it appears physically on its body.
- **Paws/Limbs** - does your dog have trouble walking or is it only dragging its legs? It could be a sign of paralysis.
- **Eyes** - are there any discharge in the eyes?
- **Overall Physique** - does your dog stays active or are there any signs of weakness and deterioration?

Teacup Yorkie Care Sheet

Congratulate yourself! You are now on your way to becoming a very well-informed and pro-active Teacup Yorkie dog owner! Finishing this book is a huge milestone for you and your future or present pet, but before this ultimate guide comes to a conclusion, keep in mind the most important things you have acquired through reading this book.

This chapter will outline the summary of what you have learned, including the checklist you need to keep in mind to ensure that you and your Teacup Yorkie lived happily ever after!

Basic Teacup Yorkie Information

Pedigree: Terrier dog breed

AKC Group: Toy Group

Breed Size: Small

Height: 5 - 6 inches (5–10 cm) for females and males

Weight: average of 2 pounds; maximum of 4 pounds

Coat Length: long and straight coat can also be curly

Coat Texture: gloss, fine and silky

Color: Black and Gold, Black and Tan, Blue and Gold

Markings: Gold Mask, Tan Mask

Ears: small, V-shaped and erect

Tail: short to medium-length

Temperament: active, friendly, loyal, bold, confident

Strangers: may be wary around strangers

Other Dogs: generally good with other dogs if properly trained and socialized; may tend to launched itself to larger dogs

Other Pets: friendly with other pets but if not properly introduce may result to potential aggression

Training: intelligent and can be trained

Exercise Needs: very active; doesn't require regular or excessive amount of exercise

Health Conditions: generally healthy but predisposed to patellar luxation, PSS, cataracts, retinal detachment, dry eye, corneal dystrophy, keratitis, hypoglycemia, and progressive retinal atrophy

Lifespan: average 12 years

Habitat Requirements

Recommended Accessories: crate, dog bed, food/water dishes, toys, collar, leash, harness, grooming supplies

Collar and Harness: sized by weight

Grooming Supplies: soft brittle brush, nail clipper

Grooming Frequency: occasional brushing; professional grooming at least 2 times a year

Energy Level: relatively high

Exercise Requirements: at least once a day plus active playtime

Crate: highly recommended

Crate Size: just large enough for dog to lie down and turn around comfortably

Crate Extras: lined with blanket or plush pet bed

Food/Water: preferably stainless steel or ceramic bowls

Toys: start with an assortment, see what the dog likes; include some mentally stimulating toys

Training: play games to give your dog extra exercise during the day; train your dog for various dog sports

Nutritional Needs

Nutritional Needs: water, protein, carbohydrate, fats, vitamins, minerals

Calorie Needs: varies by age, weight, and activity level; RER modified with activity level

Amount to Feed (puppy): feed freely but consult recommendations on the package preferably 3 – 6 times a day.

Amount to Feed (adult): consult recommendations on the package; calculated by weight

Important Ingredients: fresh animal protein (chicken, beef, lamb, turkey, eggs), digestible carbohydrates (rice, oats, barley), animal fats

Important Minerals: calcium, phosphorus, potassium, magnesium, iron, copper and manganese

Important Vitamins: Vitamin A, Vitamin A, Vitamin B-12, Vitamin D, Vitamin C

Certifications: AAFCO statement of nutritional adequacy; protein at top of ingredients list; no artificial flavors, dyes, preservatives

Breeding Information

Age of First Heat: around 7 months (or earlier)

Heat (Estrus) Cycle: 15 to 21 days

Frequency: twice a year, every 6 to 7 months

Greatest Fertility: 11 to 15 days into the cycle

Gestation Period: 58 to 68 days

Pregnancy Detection: possible after 21 days, best to wait 28 days before exam

Feeding Pregnant Dogs: maintain normal diet until week 5 or 6 then slightly increase rations

Signs of Labor: body temperature drops below normal 100° to 102°F (37.7° to 38.8°C), may be as low as 98°F (36.6°C); dog begins nesting in a dark, quiet place

Contractions: period of 10 minutes in waves of 3 to 5 followed by a period of rest

Whelping: puppies are born in 1/2 hour increments following 10 to 30 minutes of forceful straining

Puppies: born with eyes and ears closed; eyes open at 3 weeks, teeth develop at 10 weeks

Litter Size: average 1 to 5 puppies

Size at Birth: average of 2.5 ounces to 2.75 or more

Weaning: start offering puppy food soaked in water at 6 weeks; fully weaned by 8 weeks

Socialization: start as early as possible to prevent puppies from being nervous as an adult

Index

A

AAFCO..58, 116, 128
accessories 49
active 14, 114
Adenovirus 108
adopting 2, 36
age 6, 11, 19, 20, 42, 58, 82, 88, 98, 99, 100, 103, 107, 115
alpha dog..67
American Kennel Club...3
antibodies..87
appearance...1, 3, 4, 5, 107
award..3

B

barking..48
bathing 73, 74, 75, 77
bed..49, 50, 115
behavior 4, 41, 68, 69, 71, 78, 83, 85
bitch..4, 5
bleeding...79, 104, 105
body...5, 6, 41
Bordatella 108
bowls 50, 52, 115
breed 1, 2, 4, 5, 6, 10, 12, 19, 21, 29, 30, 34, 35, 36, 48, 50, 57, 61, 82, 83, 84, 85, 101, 105, 106
breeder.. 22, 24, 34, 35, 36, 37, 42, 129
breeding 2, 5, 6, 34, 35, 77, 78, 82, 84, 85
brush...5
brushing..30, 74, 75, 77, 78

C

cage 4
cancer 82, 103
Canine Influenza 108
carbohydrates 55, 59, 116
care 3
carrier 49
castrate... 5
cause.. 76, 79, 98, 104, 106
chewing 48, 51
children...2, 11, 13, 66, 113
clicker training... 67
coat.. 4, 5, 6, 7, 10, 13, 30, 51, 56, 73, 75, 76, 77, 113
collar 18, 28, 51, 114
color..5, 6, 10, 13, 66, 113
coloration 6
coloring... 4
colors 6, 10, 60
colostrum 87
comb...5, 51, 74, 75
command 5
conception...84, 85
condition 5, 73
contractions 86, 87
coordination...100, 105
costs...28, 82, 128, 130
crate... 22, 47, 49, 50, 52, 70, 71, 72, 114

D

dam..4, 6
Degenerative Myelopathy 100
diagnosis..98, 100, 105
diet.. 2, 55, 56, 57, 85, 116, 129, 131
discharge 83
disease...19, 22, 78, 98, 100, 103, 104, 105, 106, 107
disorder 5
distemper 107

Distemper..108

dog bed..114

dog training..67, 69

double coat 4

E

ear...4, 6

ears 5, 10, 13, 73, 76, 77, 78, 88, 113, 117

eating...7, 41, 43

energy...12, 56, 60

Epilepsy 97

estrus cycle..82, 85

exercise..12, 47, 48, 99, 115

expense 19

eye 3

eye problems...12

eyes.. 3, 10, 44, 76, 77, 88, 117

F

face 3

fats.. 55, 56, 59, 115, 116

feeding.. 60, 61, 70, 85, 88, 130

female...3, 4, 5, 6

food 7, 28, 43, 49, 52, 55, 57, 58, 59, 60, 61, 66, 71, 82, 88, 114, 117

foot 6

G

games 48, 115

gene 3

genealogy 6

genetic 5

gestation period...84, 85

Glaucoma 101, 102

grooming 12, 28, 74, 75, 77, 78, 114

growth 6

H

habitat 2, 48

hair 3, 4, 5, 6

harness 114

health 2, 4, 27, 34, 51, 56, 57, 73, 78, 98, 130

health problems 2, 34, 78

healthy 128

heart disease 78

heat 77, 82, 83

herding 114

hip5

Hip Dysplasia 5, 98

history 104

hormone 102, 103

house 3, 4

housetraining 22, 49, 69, 71

housing 82

Hypothyroidism 102, 103

I

illness 41

ingredients 55, 58, 59, 60, 116

intelligent 11, 14, 30, 67, 114

Intervertebral Disk Disease 105

K

kennel 4

L

labor 86, 87

leash 49, 51, 83, 114

legs 5, 76

Leptospirosis 108

license 17, 18, 28, 51

licensing..17
lifespan..12
litter 7, 33, 36, 41, 82, 84, 86
longhaired 74

M

markings...6
milk..7
minerals..55, 57, 115
money...19, 82
musculoskeletal 98, 105
mutation...100

N

nails...73, 77, 79
nose 10, 76
nursing...87, 88
nutrients..55, 87, 130
nutritional needs...58

O

obedience...37
obesity...60
outer coat..7

P

pain 99, 100, 102, 105, 106
Parainfluenza 108
paralysis...101, 105, 106
parent...4, 6
Parvovirus..108
pet store...34
pets 11, 14, 30, 78, 114, 128

positive reinforcement 67, 68

pregnant...82, 84

Progressive Retinal Atrophy 106

pros and cons 29

protein... 55, 56, 58, 59, 60, 85, 115, 116

punishment 67, 68

pupil...102

puppies..5, 7, 8, 42

puppy..... 2, 22, 24, 28, 33, 34, 35, 36, 41, 42, 43, 44, 50, 52, 61, 65, 67, 69, 70, 71, 72, 87, 88, 107, 115, 117, 128, 129, 130

puppy mills 34, 37

puppy-proofing 33, 130

purebred...3, 37

Q

quick 79

R

rabies 18, 19

record 6

registry..3

rescue 36

reward 67, 68, 71, 78

S

seizures...97, 98

shed 75

show 3

showing 2

signs 41

sire 4, 6

size 12, 20, 22, 50, 51, 61, 84

skin..4, 6, 27, 51, 56, 66, 73, 75, 76, 102, 103

skull..3

socialization...11, 65, 69 spay..5

stimulation 12, 48

supplies... 44, 49, 52, 74, 75, 79, 114

surgery...6, 105

symptoms... 99, 101, 102, 103, 105, 107

T

tail..4, 5, 76

teeth...3, 73, 77, 78, 117

temperament 1

temperature..86, 117

thyroid gland 102, 103

tips 33, 36, 47, 52, 129

toxic 44, 61

toys 28, 43, 48, 50, 52, 114, 115

train 115

training 11, 37, 67, 68, 69, 70

treatment 2, 101, 102, 103, 106

treats 27, 66

trim 5

trimming..4

types 47, 82

U

undercoat..4

undercoat rake...51, 75

urine marking..83

uterus 84, 85

V

vaccination 18

veterinarian... 28, 61, 85, 87, 100, 104

vitamins 55, 56, 115, 131

von Willebrand Factor 104

Von Willebrand's Disease 104

vulva 83

W

water 44, 49, 50, 52, 57, 59, 71, 76, 88, 114, 115, 117
weaned 43
weight... 60, 85, 98, 103, 114, 115
whelping 86, 88
whelping box...86
wire pin brush 51, 75

Photo Credits

Page 1 Photo ron.aguilar@gmail.com By via Flickr.com, <https://www.flickr.com/photos/ronaguilar/9667145214/in/photolist>

Page 10 Photo By Swatjester via Wikimedia Commons, <https://commons.wikimedia.org/wiki/File:Teacupyorkie2.jpg>

Page 17 Photo By Mike via Flickr.com, <https://www.flickr.com/photos/basicallyadvanced/8061183536/>

Page 34 Photo By deb@deb-gray.com Gray via Flickr.com, <https://www.flickr.com/photos/debgray/4990755753/>

Page 47 Photo By Swatjester via Wikimedia Commons, <https://commons.wikimedia.org/wiki/File:Teacupyorkie.jpg>

Page 54 Photo By jj.sheets via Flickr.com, <https://www.flickr.com/photos/11249990@N06/4249116610/>

Page 64 Photo By Marcia O'Connor via Flickr.com, <https://www.flickr.com/photos/97477873@N00/13002175833/>

Page 73 Photo By Callie Reed via Flickr.com,
<https://www.flickr.com/photos/machineisorganic/34875239
20/>

Page 81 Photo By John Mayer via Flickr.com,
<https://www.flickr.com/photos/johnmichaelmayer/2726465
195/>

Page 89 Photo By Ginny Baker via Flickr.com,
<https://www.flickr.com/photos/ginnylou/11662958486/>

Page 110 Photo By Swatjester via Wikimedia Commons,
<https://commons.wikimedia.org/wiki/File:Teacupyorkieupc
lose.jpg>

References

"AAFCO Dog Food Nutrient Profiles"
DogFoodAdvisor.com
<http://www.dogfoodadvisor.com/frequently-asked-questions/aafco-nutrient-profiles/>

"About Teacup Yorkies" The Nest
<http://pets.thenest.com/teacup-yorkies-4204.html>

"Annual Dog Care Costs" PetFinder.com
<https://www.petfinder.com/pet-adoption/dog-adoption/annual-dog-care-costs/>

"Choosing a Healthy Puppy" WebMD
<http://pets.webmd.com/dogs/guide/choosing-healthy-puppy>

"How to Find a Responsible Breeder" HumaneSociety.org
<http://www.humanesociety.org/issues/puppy_mills/tips/finding_responsible_dog_breeder.html?referrer=https://www.google.com/>

"My Bowl: What Goes into a Balanced Diet for Your Dog?" PetMD.com <http://www.petmd.com/dog/slideshows/ nutrition-center/my-bowl-what-goes-into-a-balanced-diet- for-your-dog>

"Nutrients Your Dog Needs" ASPCA.org <https://www.aspca.org/pet-care/dog-care/nutrients-your- dog-needs>

"Nutrition: General Feeding Guidelines for Dogs" VCAAnimalHospitals.com <http://www.vcahospitals.com/main/pet-health- information/article/animal-health/nutrition-general- feeding-guidelines-for-dogs/6491>

"Pet Care Costs" ASPCA.org <https://www.aspca.org/adopt/pet-care-costs>

"Puppy Proofing Your Home" Hill's Pet.com <http://www.hillspet.com/dog-care/puppy-proofing-your- home.html>

"Puppy Proofing Your Home" PetEducation.com <http://www.peteducation.com/article.cfm?c=2+2106&aid= 3283>

"Teacup Yorkie: The Pocket-Sized Yorkshire Terrier"
Terribly Terrier

<https://terriblyterrier.com/teacup-yorkie/>

 "What Are Teacup Yorkies, Miniature Yorkshire Terriers,
Mini, Micro & Toy Yorkies?" TeacupYorkies

<http://www.teacupyorkies.info/>

Feeding Baby
Cynthia Cherry
978-1941070000

Axolotl
Lolly Brown
978-0989658430

Dysautonomia, POTS
Syndrome
Frederick Earlstein
978-0989658485

Degenerative Disc
Disease Explained
Frederick Earlstein
978-0989658485

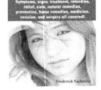

Sinusitis, Hay Fever,
Allergic Rhinitis Explained
Frederick Earlstein
978-1941070024

Wicca
Riley Star
978-1941070130

Zombie Apocalypse
Rex Cutty
978-1941070154

Capybara
Lolly Brown
978-1941070062

Eels As Pets
Lolly Brown
978-1941070167

Scabies and Lice Explained
Frederick Earlstein
978-1941070017

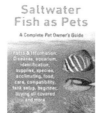

Saltwater Fish As Pets
Lolly Brown
978-0989658461

Torticollis Explained
Frederick Earlstein
978-1941070055

Kennel Cough
Lolly Brown
978-0989658409

Physiotherapist, Physical
Therapist
Christopher Wright
978-0989658492

Rats, Mice, and Dormice
As Pets
Lolly Brown
978-1941070079

Wallaby and Wallaroo Care
Lolly Brown
978-1941070031

Bodybuilding Supplements
Explained
Jon Shelton
978-1941070239

Demonology
Riley Star
978-19401070314

Pigeon Racing
Lolly Brown
978-1941070307

Dwarf Hamster
Lolly Brown
978-1941070390

Cryptozoology
Rex Cutty
978-1941070406

Eye Strain
Frederick Earlstein
978-1941070369

Inez The Miniature Elephant
Asher Ray
978-1941070353

Vampire Apocalypse
Rex Cutty
978-1941070321

Printed in Great Britain
by Amazon

55606007R00088